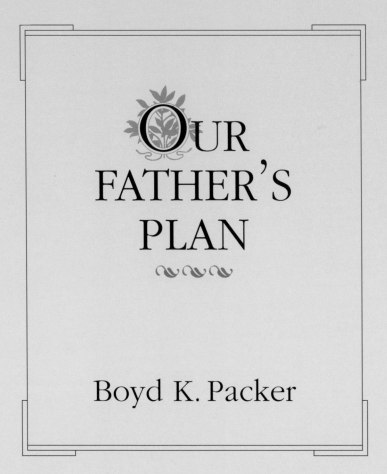

OUR FATHER'S PLAN

Boyd K. Packer

Deseret Book Company
Salt Lake City, Utah

Only Standard Works, official statements, and other
publications written under assignment from the First
Presidency and Council of the Twelve Apostles are
considered authorized publications by The Church of
Jesus Christ of Latter-day Saints.
Other publications, including this one, are the
responsibility of the writer and are not official
publications of the Church.

The Author

ISBN 0–87579–820–9
Library of Congress Catalog Card Number 84–72516

10   9   8   7   6   5   4   3   2

CONTENTS

OUR FATHER'S PLAN

Gospel principles are not always fully explained in one place in the scriptures nor presented in order or sequence. The whole plan of salvation must be assembled from pieces here and there. Sometimes one finds larger segments, but often it is in small bits scattered through the chapters and verses. Seen separately, and gathered at random, they do not easily fit together to form a plan or a chart we can follow. Nevertheless, it is essential that we look to the revelations to find the meaning of and to give direction to our lives.

After teaching Church history for a number of years, I discovered a principle that is little mentioned in textbooks of learning. I rejoiced to see how much more my students learned when the principle was applied. Thereafter, for the most part, they could move through the periods of history without being lost. They knew how to fit together the factual material they received and make it useful in their own lives.

My only regret is that this discovery was made near the end of my teaching career rather than at the beginning of it. How much more I might have taught, how much more my students might have learned, if that insight had come earlier.

This brief book, designed to be read conveniently in one sitting, is a result of that experience. It has a very specific purpose. It is the product of years of work. The brevity of it is precisely why it took so long. Refined substance combined with brevity are very difficult indeed to achieve.

What I had discovered was this: there is great value at the beginning of a course to receive a relatively brief, but very carefully organized, overview of the entire course from beginning to end.

Then the class can start at the beginning again and repeat the very same course, this time at greater length and in much more detail. The second time they go over the material, the light of learning shines more brightly because of the perspective that is gained.

In the case of those Church history classes, the preview took five class periods only, and the second journey more than a hundred. Nevertheless, those beginning periods, so brief an investment of time by comparison, enhanced to a very great measure the detailed study of the course. The preview was more than worth the time and work invested in it.

Because of the preview, the second journey may lack the excitement of a novel with a surprise ending or of a mystery to be solved in the last chapter. But this deficiency, if it is one at all, is more than balanced by the security of knowing where we are at any given time, what is to be our final destination, and how we may best move toward it.

Let me illustrate. Suppose you are to guide a group in a bus tour across a continent. A part of your preparation includes a quick plane trip over the route to gain a feeling, an insight, for the journey.

As you move swiftly above the landscape, you have a sweeping view of the continent and can see the great expanse on either side. While you do not see much detail, you have an overview of your course that you could obtain in no other way. You return with a feel for what lies ahead as you retrace that route on the ground. You now have a perspective. This may be your single most important qualification as you go once more over the same course on the ground.

There comes to be fixed in your mind a plan, a map for the journey. For the moment, it is only in broad outline form. Nevertheless, at any point in the journey you will know in general terms what stretches out ahead.

The rivers and mountains that await you will have been clearly marked on this map in your mind. Consciously or unconsciously, you will

As you move swiftly above the landscape, you have an overview of your course that you could obtain in no other way.

be making preparations for the crossings you must make. You will know as well what lies beyond the horizon on either side. Should there be deserts that might consume you, you can avoid them or cross them on a chosen route that is safe.

What a privilege it is on the second journey to be able to stop at leisure, to take side trips, or to linger here or there to explore and learn. There is great joy in learning, really learning, at one's own deliberate pace. How much that learning is improved when you understand the purpose for being there and have been given a preview of the course you are to follow.

When you know something of the destination, you know how long it is safe to linger along the way. You know also those things which,

When you know something of the destination, you know how long it is safe to linger along the way.

however interesting, are not worthy of much attention. You recognize those paths which, however enticing, however tempting, must be avoided at all cost. You will know as well those paths which must be followed regardless of difficulty.

It was this principle of a preview that served so well in the teaching of Church history. When students were given a brief, sweeping overview of the course before we trudged over it step by step, thereafter they were not lost. They could fit together the things they learned and file ideas away for future reference.

I wondered over the years how this very principle might be applied to the learning of the doctrines of the gospel. That is a different journey from Church history, where the sequence

of events provides organization and an order to follow. There is a very different challenge in learning principles of the gospel.

This book is an attempt to draw in sweeping outline form the Plan of Redemption, the course that each must follow. It is an effort to present the essential truths each of us must know if we are to move safely through life. Thereafter, separate principles, truths, and ideals gathered at random may be fitted into the plan.

If we are given a proper perspective, we can never be truly lost. Everything we learn, every truth we discover will thereafter fit somewhere into the plan.

Once we have the outline of the plan well in mind, each of us, individually, must sketch in, line by line, the details large and small. We must each add colors of our own to the individual record we will keep of the journey through mortality.

What follows was put together in the way that it is presented for a purpose. It was meant to be brief yet inclusive. It was meant to be read more than once.

Will you move, then, in your mind's eye, to some pinnacle far beyond where mortal man could fly, where one can see beyond the limits of earth and time and space. We can do that in our minds, if we will. Then we will unfold the plan. We will trace, as best we can, if only in outline form, the whole of the journey of man in mortality.

The plan we shall review is the master plan for the work of the Lord. It is our Father's plan. It is called in the scriptures the Plan of Salvation, the Plan of Redemption. He prepared it; we are to follow it.

This review of that plan will provide but a sweeping glance across the unfolded scroll of scriptural truths that have been given to us by revelation.

As we look about us from this lofty place to which we have come in our mind's eye, we can see into the heavens and sense what has transpired in the past, what is the meaning of the present, and what lies in the future.

Three shapes emerge to represent the grand divisions in the Plan of Salvation. They are circles of truth. For the scriptures define truth to be a "knowledge of things as they are, and as they were, and as they are to come." (D&C 93:24.)

There comes to us an impression of things as they were—

THE
PREMORTAL
EXISTENCE

of things as they are now,

MORTALITY

and of things as they are to be in the future,

LIFE
BEYOND THE
GRAVE

Within these three epochs of truth rest all that we know of the Plan of Salvation. They encompass all that is taught in the scriptures and in the temple endowment—indeed, all that has been revealed to us.

Three scriptural phrases emerge, the longest of them only eight words, and will quickly bring to mind the plan.

PREMORTAL EXISTENCE: *"Behold, here am I, send me."*

MORTALITY: *"This is My Beloved Son. Hear Him!"*

And of LIFE BEYOND THE GRAVE: *"Enter thou into the joy of thy Lord."*

We will highlight what we know of premortal life, of mortality, and of life beyond the grave.

Our knowledge comes from the scriptures and from apostles and prophets who wrote down what they learned when the mists were moved away and the veil was drawn back so that they could see.

Most of the time the images of these great truths stand like silhouettes in our minds. Our knowledge of the premortal life is veiled, for a curtain has been drawn across our memory of that existence. But on occasions, the mists move aside and we see for an instant a feature, even a detail.

On rare occasions, we may see one or another of them in full light. Then an image as clear as a photograph registers upon our mind. We experience inspiration and receive an increase in knowledge of who we are, where we came from, why we are here.

Most of the time the images of these great truths stand like silhouettes in our minds.

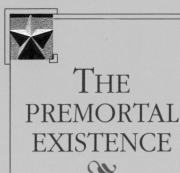

THE PREMORTAL EXISTENCE

No more profound truth has been conveyed to us in the restoration than the knowledge of our premortal existence. No other church knows or teaches this truth. The doctrine is given only in outline form, but salient facts are repeated often enough in the revelations to assure us of certain fundamental truths.

The facts are these:

We lived in the presence of God, our Eternal Father, prior to our mortal birth.

We use such words as *omnipotent* and *omniscient* to describe Him, and we feel them to be inadequate. Should not the word *God* be enough? Does it not bespeak such glory that, without the presence of priesthood power of Godliness, mortal man could not behold His face and live? (D&C 84:19–22.)

He is Elohim, our Father. The familiar word "father," reverently spoken, does not demean Him but greatly lifts us up.

The scriptures teach us that we are His offspring, His children.

They further teach that intelligence, or spirit, has existed from all eternity. (D&C 93:33; Abraham 3:22.) We know also that we were

14

individuals. We are told more than once in the revelations that we were clothed in a spirit body. (D&C 77:2.) We know no more than that the spirit body was created in the image of our Father. (Ether 3:16.)

And the most fundamental of all endowments given to us is agency. (Moses 4:3; D&C 29:35.)

To repeat, the few crucial facts we know about our status in premortal life are these: "Man was also in the beginning with God." (D&C 93:29.) We lived in the presence of God, our Eternal Father; we are His offspring. Intelligence, or spirit, was organized as spirit bodies before the world was. (See Abraham 3:22.) Each of us was endowed with agency. Authority was conferred and leaders were chosen. (Alma 13:1–4.)

From the scriptures we read: "God saw these souls that they were good, and he stood in the midst of them, and he said: These I will make my rulers; for he stood among those that

We lived in the presence of God, our Eternal Father; we are His offspring.

were spirits, and he saw that they were good." (Abraham 3:23.)

In the words of the Prophet Joseph Smith: "God Himself, finding he was in the midst of spirits and glory, because he was more intelligent, saw proper to institute laws whereby the rest could have a privilege to advance like himself." (*Teachings of the Prophet Joseph Smith*, p. 354.)

We know little more than this of what our condition was then. Nor does it serve any useful purpose to speculate or wrest the scriptures, seeking after mysteries. There is scarcely time to master the plain and precious truths revealed to guide us through mortality.

We have also, only in outline form, the record of some events that occurred in premortal times.

THE COUNCIL IN HEAVEN   We know that God the Father had a plan. We know that He called a council. We know something of what transpired and what the outcome was.

We were present during that grand council. God the Father announced the plan. It provided that we, His spirit children, already endowed with agency, would each have the opportunity to receive a body of flesh and bone and would be made free to choose between good and evil—we would be tested. Through the test we would retain, as the

Apostle Paul said, a "hope of eternal life, which God, that cannot lie, promised before the world began." (Titus 1:2.)

Two spirits arose in that council. The first, a glorious spirit, offered to fulfill the purposes of the plan and asked no recompense.

The second, a "son of the morning" (Isaiah 14:12) who was "in authority in the presence of God" (D&C 76:25), would redeem all. He would do it by compulsion and would deny the spirits agency. He demanded as recompense that the glory be given him.

The Father chose the first, and the other rebelled. When the war was over, Lucifer "was cast out into the earth, and his angels were cast

When the war was over, Lucifer "was cast out into the earth."

out with him." (Revelation 12:9.) He did not receive a temporal body. He was an unclean spirit. He became the tempter, the evil one.

THE
CREATION
Obedient to the plan, they—that is, the Gods—organized matter in the epoch known as the Creation. (Abraham 4:1.) It is described in Genesis, in the Pearl of Great Price, and in the endowment.

The light was divided from the darkness. The waters were gathered together and dry land appeared. The earth brought forth plants of every kind, each bearing seed within itself. Living creatures of every kind were created and blessed to bring forth, each after its own kind. A garden was planted eastward in Eden.

When all of this was done, God pronounced all of it to be good, very good. (Moses 2:25, 31.) Then, as required in the plan, came the crowning creation: "And I, God, created man in mine own image, in the image of mine only Begotten created I him; male and female created I them." (Moses 2:27.)

Temporal bodies were organized for Adam and Eve, and their spirits entered their bodies. They were placed in the garden and commanded to multiply and replenish the earth, a commandment they could not keep while there.

The Lord "planted the tree of life also in the midst of the garden, and also the tree of knowledge of good and evil." (Moses 3:9.) Of every tree Adam and Eve could freely partake, save the tree of knowledge of good and evil. Although they were commanded not to partake, they had their agency. They were told: "Thou mayest choose for thyself, for it is given thee; but, remember that I forbid it, for in the day that thou eatest thereof thou shalt surely die." (Moses 3:17.)

Satan beguiled Eve with half-truths, and she partook of the tree of knowledge of good and evil. (Moses 4:10–12.)

Whatever else occurred, for whatever purpose, Adam was left to decide; his agency was protected. The entire plan depended upon choice, upon decision, upon volition. "Adam fell that men might be; and men are, that they might have joy." (2 Nephi 2:25.)

"I, God, created man in mine own image, in the image of mine only Begotten created I him; male and female created I them." Temporal bodies were organized for Adam and Eve. Their spirits entered their bodies, and they were placed in the garden.

THE FALL The law had been broken; the penalty was decreed and quickly meted out: "Wherefore, I, the Lord God, caused that he [Adam] should be cast out from the Garden of Eden, from my presence, because of his transgression, wherein he became spiritually dead, which is the first death." (D&C 29:41.)

With the Fall came the first spiritual penalty— spiritual death!

Death is a separation. The separation of Adam and of his posterity from the presence of God constituted spiritual death, for it separated them from all things spiritual.

There is another death, temporal death, which is the separation of the body from the spirit.

The penalty for transgression was that, with the Fall, Adam and his posterity became subject to both deaths.

Adam was cast out of the garden because of his transgression, and "he became spiritually dead, which is the first death." There is another death, temporal death, which is the separation of the body from the spirit.

The law had been broken and justice was upheld. But mercy would appeal. Mercy won a stay of temporal death, and a probation was granted to man. (D&C 29:42.)

But temporal death was only delayed, for justice cannot be robbed, even by mercy. "It was not expedient that man should be reclaimed from this temporal death, for that would destroy the great plan of happiness." (Alma 42:8.) What we see as the end of one season, in the eternal realm of things is only the beginning of another season.

Even mercy could not waive repentance nor the ordinances essential to redemption. The part that mercy won was that a redemption could occur at all.

A probationary time was granted "that they should not die as to the temporal death, until I, the Lord God, should send forth angels to declare unto them repentance and redemption, through faith in the name of mine Only Begotten Son." (D&C 29:42.)

It was an essential part of the plan in the very beginning that we are to be taught the gospel of salvation.

The creation was complete. Mortality had come.

To man, death is the final destruction of body and spirit. In our Father's plan, it is but the beginning of another season.

MORTALITY

So it was that Adam and Eve left Eden. They ventured forth into mortality, the probationary state, Adam with Eve, his helpmeet, at his side. They were to have dominion over the earth and subdue it, to till the ground by the sweat of their brows.

Within their mortal bodies were their spirits. It was through things they would *feel* within that they had communication with that world of spirits from which they were now separated and considered dead.

They carried within their bodies the power to reproduce after their own kind. This was a divine gift. The covenant of marriage and the institution of the family were revealed to them. They could now keep the commandment to multiply and replenish the earth. Other spirits came to quicken mortal bodies prepared for them. The love of a father and a mother whispers of a greater heritage than mortal eyes can see. (Moses 5:10–12.)

The mortal body is the instrument of our mind and the foundation of our character. Through it we are tested. The sacred power of procreation gives us an essential part in the plan. There are laws, eternal laws, set to govern our use of it. It

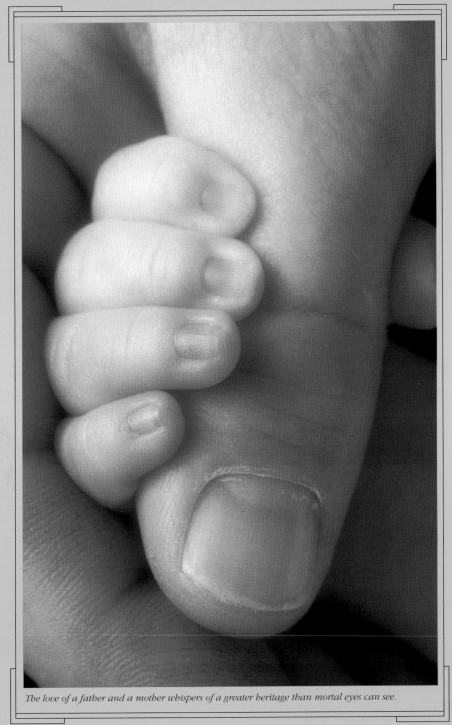

The love of a father and a mother whispers of a greater heritage than mortal eyes can see.

The heavens were opened and the Plan of Redemption was given to mankind.

is to operate in very narrow limits. And there are penalties of eternal consequence if we disobey.

There is also the ever-present tempter. "Because he had fallen from heaven, and had become miserable forever, he sought also the misery of all mankind." (2 Nephi 2:18.) He and his angels tempt us to degrade or misuse this and every other sacred gift we have received. He is determined to have us serve him, and conspires to replace every feeling of love with one that is corrupt.

Agency requires that we be free to use the power as we will. The laws of nature provide that every time the natural conditions are met, whether under the bonds of marriage or not, a

body will be conceived and a spirit assigned. But who, knowing of the Plan of Salvation, could think of misusing the power of procreation?

The teaching of the Plan of Salvation, the doctrine of the Kingdom of God, became preeminent among the commandments of God. The heavens were opened and the Plan of Redemption was given. Angelic messengers were sent and prophets were commissioned to teach mankind of their beginnings with God.

Without a knowledge of the gospel plan, transgression seems natural, innocent, even justified. There is no greater protection from the adversary than for us to know the truth—to know the plan!

Divine power and authority interceded! The world was washed clean.

And, there is the Holy Spirit. The Spirit is our tie to that realm from which we came. It always works by persuasion, never by compulsion, never by force.

The history of mankind records that man multiplied and scattered abroad on the face of the earth. Mankind turned aside from the counsel of the prophets of God. The tempter prevailed and gained such control that, during the time of Noah, there was scarcely a place fit to receive the spirits awaiting their turn on earth. With the exception of eight souls, the people on earth lost the Holy Spirit and rejected the plan.

The last cleansing, which has been foretold by prophets, will be by fire.

Divine power and authority interceded! The world was washed clean, saving only seed to begin it all again— Noah and his family.

This baptism foreshadowed another cleansing that is to come. The last cleansing, as foretold by the prophets, will be by fire. But this will not come until the purposes of the Lord have been fulfilled. For, while Satan has power to bruise the heel, the seed of woman shall have power to bruise his head. (Moses 4:21.)

The purpose for coming into mortality is twofold: spirits come to receive a body, and each is tested against both good and evil preparatory to reentering the presence of our Father.

Over us always and continually hangs the specter of temporal death, the separation of the body and the spirit, which death is the grave. (2 Nephi 9:11.) The temporal death, although mercifully delayed for a time of probation, will surely come. We will be separated from our mortal bodies.

If there were no more to the plan, should it have ended there, the purposes of God would be frustrated. Our bodies would be lost forever.

Jacob explained that "this flesh must have laid down to rot and to crumble to its mother earth, to rise no more. . . . Our spirits must become subject to that angel who fell from the presence of the Eternal God. . . . And our spirits must have become like unto him." (2 Nephi 9:7–9.)

If the plan had provided only for the resurrection of the temporal body, an unclean spirit would reunite with the body. We could not return to the presence of God. The result would be spiritual death. Seven times in explicit brevity the scriptures state that "no unclean thing can dwell with God." (1 Nephi 10:21.)

Obedient to the plan, He Himself received His body from mortal woman.

Consider our plight. Because of the testing, each of us, to one degree or another, becomes unclean. Without a way to cleanse ourselves, we would remain forever spiritually dead and forever subject to the evil one.

But there is more to the plan, for it is the Plan of Redemption. The coming of a Savior, a Redeemer, is the central message of the scriptures and is stated as simply as this: "The Messiah cometh in the fulness of time, that he may redeem the children of men from the fall." (2 Nephi 2:26.) To quote Jacob again, "O how great the plan of our God!" (2 Nephi 9:13.)

Awaiting His turn in the premortal sphere was the Christ, the Redeemer. It is with the deepest reverence that we recite something of the purpose of His ministry on earth.

Obedient to the plan, He Himself received His body from mortal woman. He was the Only Begotten Son of God in the flesh.

When the day came that had been foretold by the prophets, no wonder that choirs of angels sang and there were great signs in the heaven.

He experienced mortal life much as other men. He taught His gospel of faith, repentance, baptism, and the laying on of hands for the gift of the Holy Ghost. He taught us to pray, revealed the ordinances, and bestowed His authority. He organized His church.

Although He was innocent and clean every whit, He was rejected, betrayed, and condemned to mortal death.

But with Him, there is a difference. He is the Only Begotten Son of God. Man cannot of himself choose to live, for man has no power over death. But Christ possessed the power of life, and He need not choose to die. Volition, decision, *agency:* these are central to the plan.

His death, His sacrifice had to be by His own choice.

There is no more majestic moment in the history of the world than when Christ stood before Pilate and was told, "Knowest thou not that I have power to crucify thee, and have power to

release thee?" His answer: "Thou couldest have no power at all against me, except it were given thee from above." (John 19:10–11.)

Christ chose to die. He accepted the penalty for our transgressions to satisfy justice if we would but repent, for the law of justice cannot be broken; otherwise God would cease to be God.

Christ went below all things so that He might rise above all things. He was pure and without blemish. He had no part with the adversary. Therefore He could reenter the presence of God. What happened in Gethsemane and at Golgotha satisfied the law. He atoned for the transgressions of mankind, a supernal expression of mercy.

Just how the Atonement was wrought, we do not know. But thereafter, the Resurrection began, and eventually all mankind will reclaim their bodies.

With the atoning sacrifice of Jesus Christ, the terrible specter of the eternal death of the body no longer hovers over us. We are redeemed from temporal death, which death is the grave. Jesus Christ offered resurrection without condition and without cost. This restoration comes to all, the just and the unjust. Otherwise man would be punished for Adam's transgression, and injustice would prevail.

But redemption from spiritual death, from hell,

Baptism must be by immersion, for it is symbolic of both the coming forth from temporal death, from the grave, and the cleansing required for redemption from spiritual death.

is another matter. For this, conditions are set. There are requirements established that are as eternal and absolute as the laws of mercy and justice themselves. Nevertheless, the way was opened for us to become clean once more and to be eligible to return to the presence of God, if we will.

Our redemption from spiritual death can be worked out only under the conditions God has established, beginning with faith in the Lord Jesus Christ and repentance. Covenants and ordinances are required. Baptism by immersion for the remission of sins is the first ordinance.

Baptism must be by immersion, for it is symbolic of both the coming forth from temporal death, from the grave, and the cleansing required for redemption from spiritual death.

To complete the remission of sins, baptism is followed by the laying on of hands for the gift of the Holy Ghost. (See 2 Nephi 31:17 and D&C 19:31.) Under the plan, baptism is not just for

Baptism is followed by the laying on of hands for the gift of the Holy Ghost.

Through the sacrament we renew the covenant of baptism.

entrance into the Church of Jesus Christ. It begins a spiritual rebirth that may eventually lead back into the presence of God.

If we really understood what baptism signifies, we could never consider it trivial nor alter the form of this sacred ordinance. When we accept the principles and the ordinances of the gospel, repentance and baptism, and become spiritually alive, we may receive forgiveness for our sins through repentance without repeated baptisms. Through the sacrament we renew the covenant.

We have the hope that we can retain a remission of our sins. If we are obedient to the laws and ordinances of the gospel, we may look forward with hope, having faith in Christ, to life beyond the veil.

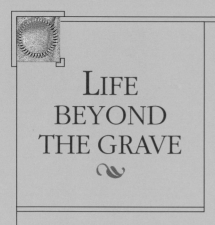

LIFE
BEYOND
THE GRAVE

Our knowledge of life beyond the veil, like our knowledge of the premortal life, is given to us only in outline form. But salient facts are repeated in the scriptures, and we are given sufficient doctrine to know what we must do to prepare for it.

As with our knowledge of the premortal life, there is little to be gained by seeking after the mysteries, for there is hardly time in a lifetime to master the plain and precious things. The facts we know are these:

When we die as to mortality, the spirit leaves the body and is taken to a place of rest. Just as Eden was a place between the premortal world and mortality, so there is prepared a place between temporal death and our return to the presence of God.

Those persons who are righteous are taken to paradise.

Those persons who are wicked are consigned to a spirit prison.

Justice will be upheld to the very letter of the law and demands that no one of us can be redeemed without the ordinances. That same justice requires that those who were denied a knowledge of the Plan of Salvation upon the earth will have the gospel preached to them. The dead must have the opportunity to receive the ordinances. They can repent and make covenants, if they will.

Justice, so often feared by man, is in truth a friend, a protector.

The essential ordinances of the gospel that they did not receive in mortality (baptism, ordination to the priesthood, the endowment, the sealing ordinance) will be vicariously provided for them. Justice, so often feared by man, is in truth a friend, a protector.

Mercy is revealed in full tenderness and in the commandment that we, the living, vicariously do for the dead what they cannot do for themselves. Those who do this work on earth have a crucial part in the plan.

There is yet another death, a second spiritual death, which will be pronounced only upon the sons of perdition.

Beyond the veil we will await a judgment, the resurrection, and thereafter the final judgment. We will be called forth from paradise or from prison to inherit, after the final judgment, that degree of glory that we merit, that which we have earned.

There is yet another death, a second spiritual death, which will be pronounced only upon the sons of perdition who have "denied the Holy Spirit after having received it, and [have] denied the Only Begotten Son of the Father, having crucified him unto themselves and put him to an open shame." They are "the only ones on whom the second death shall have any power." (D&C 76:35, 37.) After the resurrection, they shall be cast into outer darkness.

We may, if we have been worthy, come forth in the morning of the first resurrection. If we have been true and faithful in all things, we shall approach the veil and there, with signs and tokens given, we will be extended the sublimest of all invitations: "Enter into the joy of thy Lord."

An exaltation awaits each of us who is worthy to receive it. We shall receive celestial, terrestrial, or telestial bodies in the resurrection.

Those who inherit the celestial glory shall possess bodies like unto the Father, bodies that have a glory akin to the glory of the sun. Our memory of premortal life will be restored in perfect clarity.

"The glory of the celestial is one, even as the glory of the sun is one. And the glory of the terrestrial is one, even as the glory of the moon is one. And the glory of the telestial is one, even as the glory of the stars is one." (Doctrine and Covenants 76:96–98.)

To be worthy of exaltation in the presence of God and enjoy association with our own family is to receive the consummate of all blessings that God has provided in His plan.

If we have been endowed and sealed and have kept our covenants, we will assemble with our families. There is also the promise of eternal increase.

The doctrine of the eternal nature of family ties is neither known nor taught elsewhere in Christianity. To be worthy of exaltation in the presence of God and enjoy association with our own family is to receive the consummate of all blessings that God has provided in His plan.

What happens thereafter, we do not know; more than this we have not been given. But in due time, if we

Much of the knowledge that was revealed to ancient prophets was lost.

are righteous, we shall know, for unto those who are righteous, the Father will "reveal all mysteries," even the "wonders of eternity." (D&C 76:7–8.)

If we are righteous, all that the Father hath shall be given us (D&C 84:38), for we shall be gods.

With each of us, the resurrection is a certainty.

For each of us, our degree of exaltation awaits the test.

A knowledge of the plan came to the Church through holy men of God who spake as they were moved upon by the Holy Ghost. It was revealed in the dispensations of the gospel—epoch periods in which portions of the plan were unfolded.

Then came the restoration!

Those dispensations, one following after another, moved toward the final one, the dispensation of the fulness of times.

Much of the knowledge revealed to ancient prophets and that which was given during the ministry of Christ upon the earth was lost.

Then came the restoration!

After the dark ages of apostasy, when the final dispensation came, God the Father Himself, accompanied by the Son, announced it. He introduced as an echo of the grand council in heaven, "This is My Beloved Son. Hear Him!" (Joseph Smith–History 1:17.)

The morning breaks, the shadows flee;
Lo, Zion's standard is unfurled!
The dawning of a brighter day
Majestic rises on the world.

The Only Begotten Son of God, our Elder Brother, would oversee the restoration of the gospel, of the Plan of Salvation.

The Lord placed the administration of His plan into the hands of chosen men who were called, ordained, and organized. The men He chose, beginning with Joseph Smith, were given the keys to the Kingdom of God upon the earth.

They were ordained as apostles, as prophets, seers, and revelators! He brought from generations past those who last held authority and had them confer it.

The Aaronic Priesthood, which is the preparatory priesthood, was restored to us. The Melchizedek Priesthood, or the Holy Priesthood after the order of the Son of God, was restored to us. He arranged a procedure for succession by which authority is conveyed from one generation to another, without interruption, until the plan is consummated.

And the Lord appeared again to introduce Elijah the prophet, who bestowed the keys of the sealing power.

Such knowledge of the Plan of Salvation as remained in the Old Testament and the New Testament was not a fulness. There came, as a voice from the dust, the testimony of other ancient prophets—the Book of Mormon, Another

Testament of Jesus Christ. It contains the fulness of the gospel. It is a supernal gift and is the cornerstone of our religion. From it we have a knowledge of the Plan of Salvation.

Christ reopened the channels of revelation. The Doctrine and Covenants and the Pearl of Great Price were given. And He adds from time to time, by revelation, further light and knowledge. In our day, new revelations have been added to the scriptures.

He has revealed all of the principles, laws, doctrines, covenants, and ordinances required for the salvation and exaltation of man. All of this has been restored by revelation and has been bestowed in successive visitations from beyond the veil.

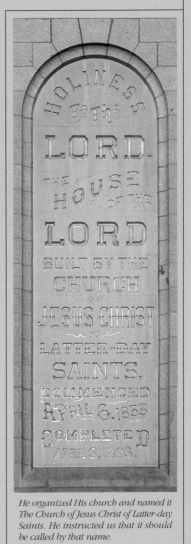

He organized His church and named it The Church of Jesus Christ of Latter-day Saints. He instructed us that it should be called by that name.

He organized His church and named it The Church of Jesus Christ of Latter-day Saints. He instructed us that it should be called by that name.

THE MISSION OF THE CHURCH

❧

And so in our day, we who are members of His church have taken upon ourselves by consecration the obligation to serve Him.

A three-fold mission has been given to the Church. First, we are to preach the gospel to every nation, kindred, tongue, and people. Then we are to persuade them to repent. We are to convert them from the ways of the world and from apostate doctrines. And when they repent, we are authorized to administer the ordinance of baptism and confer upon them the gift of the Holy Ghost. This is the work of preaching.

"For behold the field is white already to harvest." (Doctrine and Covenants 4:4.)

Thereafter we are to teach them obedience to all of the laws and ordinances of the new and everlasting covenant, which is the gospel. We are to worthily enter into the covenant of marriage and provide temporal bodies for spirits to enter mortality.

We are to prepare the posterity of Adam in all things to enter the presence of God. This is the labor of perfecting the saints.

We are to receive the baptism of water and of the Spirit for and in behalf of those who have died without the knowledge of the truth (D&C 128:5), and be ordained, endowed, and sealed for them vicariously. This is our bond, our tie to life beyond the veil. When we know the Plan of Redemption, we understand why there must

We are to preach the gospel to every nation, kindred, tongue, and people.

be a linking of all of the generations of man. This is our part in the redemption of the dead.

Through the work of preaching to the world, perfecting the saints, and redeeming the dead, we become saviors of mankind.

The Plan of Redemption, as contained in the Standard Works, must be the foundation of all that we do as members of His church. All of the elements of the plan must be retained in pure form. We must not be diverted from them. They must not be ignored or clouded or diluted or diminished or superseded by any interest that we may have. To do otherwise is to waste the days of our probation purchased for us at so great a price.

We are to teach obedience to all of the laws and ordinances of the new and everlasting covenant.

This, then, is our Father's plan. Once we understand the essentials of it, the truths revealed to us in the scriptures and the counsel given to us by the servants of the Lord begin to fit together.

In our mind's eye we have viewed the sweeping panorama of the Plan of Redemption. Let us come down now from that vantage point. Let us come back to the here and now, to our present place in mortality. Let us come find ourselves and find where we are in life.

Some of us are young, striding out with certain steps to cross the plains of mortal life. Some of us have crossed those plains already and now work our way slowly toward the summit of maturity. Some have reached that place, passed

We are to receive the baptism of water and of the Spirit for and in behalf of those who have died without the knowledge of the truth, and be ordained, endowed, and sealed for them vicariously.

over, and move, with ever slower steps, toward the end of our mortal probation.

If we have come to know our Father's plan, we are never completely lost. We know something of how it was before our mortal birth. We know much of what lies beyond the horizon on either side, and which path will be safe for us to follow. With a knowledge of the plan comes also the determination to live the principles leading to eternal life.

With that knowledge comes testimony. For we find along the way spiritual provisions of insight, courage, and direction. There are experiences that convince us that we are never alone.

We come to know through our feelings the presence of a divine providence watching over us as we move through mortality.

When we know the plan, we understand why mortality must be a test. We know why so very much must be taken on faith alone. We develop patience with the unanswered questions of life and face with greater resolution the trials and tribulations that are the lot of humankind.

When we know the plan, we know who we are, we know why we are, and we know where we are. We know that each is a son or daughter of God. One day, if we will, we may return to His presence. For this is the grand purpose of the Father and of the Son, who spoke to Moses, saying, "Behold, this is my work and my glory—to bring to pass the immortality and eternal life of man." (Moses 1:39.)

PHOTO CREDITS